Image credits: Royalty free images are reproduced under license from stock image suppliers. Images reproduced under creative commons licenses are properly noted.

D0052422

Contents

Introduction

The gold-ringed cat snake is active mostly at night when it eats mice and rats.

There are 2,900 different kinds of snakes in the world. Some snakes like boa constrictors and pythons haven't changed much since dinosaurs were alive.

There are snakes all over the world except where the ground is frozen all year. There are even snakes that live underwater.

Pythons and boa constrictors are as old as the dinosaurs.

Snakes are *reptiles*. Reptiles have scales and a backbone. Reptiles also have lungs so they can breathe on land.

Snakes don't have legs. Instead of walking, they glide along the ground or through the water.

4

Anatomy

*Even huge snakes like this Python get scared
sometimes. It hisses to warn attackers to stay away.*

Snakes don't have legs, ears or eyelids.

They don't have voices either, but snakes hiss
when they are frightened.

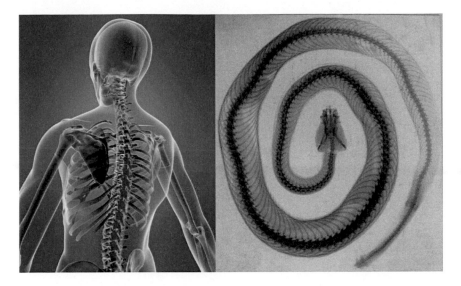

Hundreds of vertebrae make the snake's backbone very flexible compared to a person's.

All snakes are *vertebrates*. A vertebrate is an animal with a backbone. Each of a snake's vertebra has ribs attached to it.

Some snakes have over 200 vertebrae which makes them very flexible. Humans backbones only have 33 vertebrae.

Feeding

The claws of a crayfish stick out as a Queen Snake swallows it whole.

All snakes are carnivores. A carnivore is an animal that eats other animals.

Snakes eat bugs, snails, fish, frogs, mice, rats, and lizards. There are some snakes that only eat one kind of animal. The Queen Snake's favorite food is crayfish.

This lucky Parrot Snake found a frog for dinner!

The snake's lower jaw is very flexible. This allows the snake to eat things that are much bigger than the snake's mouth.

Snakes can't chew so they have to swallow their food whole. If a snake eats a big meal, it might not have to eat again for weeks or months.

Some snakes have fangs. The fangs release poison into their prey so the snake can eat it more easily.

Senses

This Grass Snake tastes the air with its forked tongue.

Snakes stick out their tongues to smell the air.
This is how they know if there is food or
predators nearby.

Most snakes have good eyesight. What they are
best at it is seeing movement.

Snakes have very sensitive stomachs. They can
feel vibrations in the ground and know how big
something is. If a person takes a step, the ground
shakes a lot. The snake will know something big
is coming. When a mouse walks, the ground

doesn't shake much at all so the snake knows there is a small animal close by.

The hole between this Red-tailed Bamboo Pit Viper's eye and nostril lets it "see" heat.

Some snakes have *pits* between their eyes and nostrils. These pits allow the snake to sense heat. This is called *infrared vision*. They can find a mouse or frog for dinner even in total darkness.

Scales And Coloring

Scales on this Green Mamba help it hide in the grass.

Snakes have scales that come in many colors.

The scales on the snake's stomach help it move. The different colored scales on the top of the snake help it hide.

The dry scales of snakes don't leave slime on your hand when you hold them.

Snake scales are smooth and dry. They aren't slimy like a worm or wet like a fish.

Defense

The harmless Milk Snake fools predators by looking like the poisonous Coral Snake.

Snakes have a lot of enemies, but they have many ways to keep from being eaten.

Most snakes blend in with their environment so they are hard to see.

Other snakes are brightly colored. The bright colors tell predators that the snake is poisonous to eat. Some snakes, like the *Milk Snake*, stay safe because they look like poisonous snakes.

This Hognosed Snake is pretending to be dead so predators leave it alone.

There are even snakes with special ways to protect themselves. The *Eastern Garter Snake* releases a stinky liquid when it is attacked. *The Hognose Snake* "plays dead" when an animal comes after it.

The most common way snakes defend themselves is to get away quick. They slide through the grass and disappear. Sometimes snakes will head for water or climb trees to escape.

14

Movement

This snake locks onto to the rocks with the scales on its stomach, then pushes itself forward.

A snake moves in a special way. First the snake "grabs" the ground with the scales near its tail. Then the snake pushes itself forward.

To move like a snake lie down on your back with your knees bent. Then push yourself forward by straightening your legs. It's hard for a person, but snakes do it easily.

This sidewinder hops across the desert sand.

Sidewinders live in slippery sand. The sand is too smooth for the snake to grab onto. So, the sidewinder hops sideways across the desert.

Molting

This California King Snake has just molted.

Scientists aren't sure why snakes shed their skin.

Some people say snakes molt when the old skin is dirty or has tiny bugs on it. Other scientists think the snake outgrows its old skin.

When a snake molts, the old skin is left behind.
Sometimes you can find them.

To shed its skin a snake rubs its head on
something rough. This makes a hole in the old
skin. Then the snake crawls out of its skin. The
old skin is like a sock that is turned inside-out.

Anacondas

Green Anacondas live in the marshes and swamps of South America.

Pound-for-pound *Anacondas* are the biggest snakes in the world. They are also one of the longest snakes and can grow up to 30 feet (10 meters) long. That's longer than a bus!

Anacondas live in the wetlands and rainforests of South America. They are cumbersome on land, but in the water anacondas are sneaky and sly.

They hunt by waiting near the top of the water for an animal to come by for a drink. Their nostrils are on top of its nose, so it can stay hidden and still breathe.

The nostrils of anacondas are on top of their snouts so the snake can breathe while hidden mostly under water.

Anacondas are a member of the *constrictor* family of snakes. Constrictors wrap around their prey and squeeze until it stops moving. Then the snake swallows its prey whole.

Because anacondas are so big, they can swallow big animals including crocodiles, wild pigs and deer. Anacondas only have to eat 5 or 6 times a year.

Boa Constrictors

This boa constrictor hides in the dark waiting to ambush its prey.

Boa constrictors are powerful snakes and very good hunters. They live in the tropics of Central and South America. They are excellent swimmers, but boa constrictors usually stay on land.

They hunt at night for rats, birds and monkeys. Boas wait silently for their prey to come by and then they attack.

Boa constrictors are related to anacondas and pythons.

Boas have sharp teeth that hold their victim long enough for the snake to wrap its body around its prey. Then the boa squeezes until the animal stops breathing and eats it headfirst.

Boas live a long time, up to 30 years. They can get as big as 100 pounds (45 kilograms) and 15 feet (5 meters) long.

Black Racers

This Black Racer smells the air with its tongue before darting away in an instant.

Black racers live throughout the United States. They aren't venomous, but racers shake their tails to sound like a rattlesnake. This fools attackers and scares them away.

Black racers are *diurnal*. Diurnal animals are active during the day. At night they rest in burrows or rock piles.

Black racers are less afraid of people than other snakes, so it's common to see them. Usually a black racer will hold perfectly still until you get too close, then it will whiz away at top speed.

This black racer hunts along the ground where it looks for moving insects and small animals.

Black racers eat insects, frogs, toads, lizards and other snakes. Black racers even eat venomous snakes like rattlesnakes and copperheads.

Black racers are very good at seeing movement. But, if their prey holds perfectly still, the snake will pass right by without seeing it.

Cobras

This cobra scares its enemies away by rising up and spreading out its hood.

Some *cobras* grow to be 18 feet (4.5 meters) long. When they are threatened, cobras raise themselves straight up off the ground. They also hiss and spread out their hoods.

Cobras live in forests and are often found near rivers. There are 270 different kinds of cobras in the world. They live in Asia, Australia, and Africa.

This young cobra got scared and spread out its hood.

Normally the cobra's hood is next to its body. But, when the cobra lifts its ribs, the hood spreads out. The cobra's hood looks like a face with huge eyes. This helps to scare attackers away.

Cobras have fangs they use to inject poison into their prey. The poison makes the animal hold still while the cobra eats it. Cobras eat lizards, frogs, birds, rodents and even other snakes. Cobras only need to eat every 2 months.

Cobras are the only snake in the world that build a nest and guard their eggs. Cobras lay about 70 eggs. The eggs take 2 months to hatch.

This cobra is coming out of a basket as a snake charmer plays music and waves his instrument.

Snake charmers play music and wave their instrument back and forth. When the charmer does this, the cobra will rise up.

Many people think the cobra hears the music, but cobras can't hear. Really, the cobra is following the movement of the instrument as the snake charmer waves it back and forth.

Copperheads

The venomous Copperhead gets its name from its orange colored head.

Copperheads live in the United States and Northern Mexico. They usually grow to be 30 inches (76 centimeters) long.

Copperheads are one of the most common venomous snakes. They usually live near marshes and swamps. Some copperheads are found on hillsides.

Like all snakes, copperheads are carnivores. Copperheads have fangs they use to inject venom into their prey. Adult copperheads eat a lot of rodents and lizards.

They bite animals like mice and then let them go. The mouse will run away with the snake's poison in it. When the mouse dies, the copperhead will track it and then eat it.

Young copperheads have a yellow tip on their tail. They wave their tails to attract prey. They eat mostly insects and caterpillars.

Copperheads don't lay eggs. Instead they give birth to live baby snakes. Usually there are 5 babies born every year. The babies are born with fangs and venom.

Garter Snakes

This Garter Snake swims easily in a pond.

Garter Snakes can be found in most of Canada and the United States. Most garter snakes are about 30 inches (73 centimeters) long. Bigger garter snakes grow up to 53 inches (135 centimeters).

Garter snakes live in underground dens during the winter. The snakes don't eat while in the den. Sometimes a den has over 200 snakes. They leave in the spring when it's warm outside.

This garter snake doesn't bite when handled gently.

Garter snakes are common and often caught by people. The snakes don't usually bite if handled carefully.

Baby garter snakes are born alive in the summertime. Young garter snakes eat mostly worms.

Adult garters like frogs, fish, tadpoles and insects. Garter snakes don't ambush their prey. They hunt by traveling through the grass and water searching for food.

Pythons

This Burmese Rock Python hunts for monkeys at night.

Burmese Rock Pythons live up to 30 years. They weigh as much as 200 pounds (90 kilograms) in the wild. Pythons grow to be 23 feet (7 meters) long. That is long enough to wrap all the way around a car!

The world's biggest snake is a python. It weighs over 400 pounds (180 kilograms) and lives in the

Serpent Safari Park in Illinois.

This python lives in the Florida Everglades where a careless pet owner let it go.

Pythons live in Asia and Africa where it is hot and wet. Some python owners let their pet pythons go in the Florida Everglades. Now these pythons survive there in the wild.

Pythons hunt at night but don't see very well. They find their food with heat-sensors and by smelling with their tongues. The python's teeth are angled so its prey can't escape once the python bites it.

Python's teeth are angled backward to hold onto their prey and never let go.

Pythons eat monkeys, lizards, antelope and springboks. Like boas and anacondas, pythons are constrictors. Constrictors squeeze their prey before swallowing.

Pythons digest their food very slowly. If they have a big meal like an antelope, they don't have to eat again for a whole year.

Female pythons usually lay around 35 eggs. Unlike most snakes, pythons stay with their eggs until they hatch. The female even wraps around her eggs to keep them warm.

Rattle Snakes

This rattlesnake is resting in the sun to warm up after a cold night.

There are 24 different kinds of rattlesnakes found in the United States, Mexico and Canada. They live in deserts, mountains and plains. All rattlesnakes have a rattle at the end of their tail.

The rattle grows one section at a time when the snake sheds its skin. The rattlesnake shakes its rattle to distract prey before it attacks. The rattle also scares enemies away.

This Black-tailed Rattlesnake has 9 rattles on its tail and is very loud.

The sound of the rattle comes from the sections of the tail banging together. The bigger the rattlesnake's tail, the louder it is.

Rattlesnakes eat rats, mice, rabbits and birds. When the rattlesnake bites its prey, poison is squeezed out of their hollow fangs into the animal.

The venom makes the animal unable to move while the snake swallows it. When not in use, the rattlesnake's fangs fold up inside its mouth.

This rattlesnake raises itself up and shakes its tail to scare predators away.

Rattlesnakes have good night vision. They also have pits that can sense heat from a live animal. This makes it easy for the rattlesnake to hunt at night.

Sometimes people or pets are bitten by rattlesnakes. The bite can be painful, but people hardly ever die from rattlesnake bites.

Sea Snakes

This Sea Snake swims to the surface to take a breath of air.

Sea snakes live on the coasts of Asia, Africa and Australia. They live their whole lives in the ocean.

Sea snakes are very curious animals. They often swim near divers to see what they are doing.

They have very poisonous venom, but they are very gentle. Sea snakes only bite people when they are mistreated.

This Sea Snake glides smoothly through the water looking for food.

The head of a sea snake is tiny. Their small head allows them to poke into little cracks and holes.

They look for eggs, fish and eels to eat. Sea snakes can hold their breath for over an hour while they search for food.

Female sea snakes give birth to 4 to 6 babies. The babies are born underwater. They quickly swim to the surface for their first breath of air.

A Note From John

Dear Reader,

Thank you very much for reading my snakes book.

Every time I write a book, I'm fascinated by what I learn. For example I had no idea that some snakes guarded their eggs. Or that cobras were the only snake that can rise straight up!

It's my hope that I can pass some of my love and enthusiasm for nature on to you and your children.

I also write in hopes that your family enjoys reading these books and talking about them together; giving you the opportunity to teach your children and grow closer as a family.

And of course, I truly hope you are inspired to appreciate this beautiful world we live in.

I get great feedback from teachers, parents and children who have enjoyed this book. I hope you liked it too!

If you did, please leave me a 5 star review on Amazon. Your review helps me out a lot and is probably the most appreciated thing you can do for me! :)

You can leave a review by using the QR code later in this book or going to:

https://www.amazon.com/review/create-review?asin=B00GV2W8JW

This snakes book is the first in a series of *Nature Books for Children*. I'm excited to write this series for you and your loved ones.

Again, if you and your children enjoyed this book, I'd like to ask you to leave a great review on Amazon. Reviews help others discover the book and I love knowing that I've given something to you and your family.

Thank you so much!

John

P.S. Feel free to write me at johnnie.yost@gmail.com

Thanks again!

P.P.S. Please visit my author page below to see what new books I have for you!

http://amazon.com/author/johnyost

Here's the QR Code to leave a review:

Photography Credits:

Although I don't have to under the creative commons license, I want to give credit to the photographers for the images in this book.

These people were kind enough to let others use their photographs, the least we can do is show them we appreciate their work and kindness. Images in order of appearance:

Gold-ringed cat snake: Thanwan Singh@flickr

Green Python: Reinhold Leitner

Python hissing: wildxplorer@flickr

Snake skeleton X-ray: otisarchives2@flickr

Queen snake with crayfish: PeteandNoeWoods@flickr

Parrot snake with frog: brian.gratwicke@flickr

Grass snake with tongue out: wikiimages public domain

Green pit viper: stevesnake shillong@filkr

Green mamba: (Kool Cats Photography)@flickr

Garter snake in hand: Ilouque@flickr

Milk snake: Jeromi Hefner@flickr

Coral snake: rarvesen@flickr

Hognosed snake playing dead: hspauldi@flickr

Garter snake crawling: Martin Cathrae@flickr

Sidewinder: G jewel is for grandma@flickr

California king snake: Tom Brandt@flickr

Snake skin: Paul Garland@flickr

Anaconda in tree: lana.japan@flickr

Anaconda: Jeff Kubina@flickr

Boa on ground: DuSantos@flickr

Boa in tree: macrodede@flickr

Black racer: purchased image

Black racer face: mbarrison@flickr

Cobra showing design on back: INeedCoffe.com@flickr

Cobra composite: Steve Slater@flickr

Cobra coming out of basket: RussBowling@flickr

Copperhead face: MrGuilt@flickr

Copperhead on ground: Jeromi Hefner@flickr

Garter snake in water: USFS Region 5@flickr

Garter in hand: Benimoto@flickr

Burmese Rock Python: wwarby@flickr

Python in Everglades: USFWS/Southeast@flickr

Python skull: Ryan Somma@flickr

Rattlesnake head and tail: Paul G Morris@flickr

Black-tailed rattler tail: eschipul@flickr

Rattler in defensive stance: David-O@flickr

Sea snake going to surface: Joi@flickr

Sea snake and coral: elias levy@flickr

Thanks for reading and enjoying "*Snakes*," the first in this *Nature Books for Children Series*!

Please check out my author page to see if there are more books you and your kids can share together!

Just type in http://amazon.com/author/johnyost

and check them out!

Something Extra for You

Just to say "Thank you" for purchasing this book, I want to give you a gift

100% absolutely free

Two beautiful "Baby Animal" wallpapers you can use as screensavers or as your desktop background.

http://naturebooksforchildren.com/free-gift/

Made in the USA
San Bernardino, CA
11 March 2019